The Prayer That Heals

The Prayer That Heals

Praying for Healing in the Family

Francis MacNutt

ave maria press AmP Notre Dame, Indiana

© 1981 by Ave Maria Press

© 2005 by Ave Maria Press, Inc.

www.avemariapress.com

Cover and text design by Andrew Borys

International Standard Book Number: 1-59471-055-4

Library of Congress Catalog Card Number: 80-69770

Library of Congress Cataloging-in-Publication Data is available.

Printed and bound in the United States of America.

Contents

Introduction

Many years ago, I first discovered, in a personal way, the amazing good news that Jesus still heals people when we pray with them and that he would even heal people through my simple prayers. In the years that followed, I learned more about the best ways of praying for the sick. Then, I started to encourage others to pray and saw them make the same glad discovery of the great love that God has for them! Nearly every day my friends and I saw remarkable healings take place. The most rewarding sight of all was to see such things as the tears of happiness glistening on the face of an elderly woman, free of pain for the first time in years, as she realized how much Jesus cared for her personally.

Then, in 1981, after the success of my first book, *Healing*, I decided to write this little book in order to encourage ordinary people to pray for healing in their families. So many people had been taught that healing was rare or that it would only happen if you were very holy (Catholics) or even that healing had ceased with the death of the last apostle (Calvinists). What we had rediscovered was healing prayer, this pearl of great price. Instead of buying it, we wished to share it—and share it gladly.

The darker side to this happy discovery of God's healing power was my growing wonderment at how Christians had come, in large measure, to lose this precious heritage of healing prayer. Some churches even question whether God heals today through anything other than natural means, such as medicine. Somehow an "enemy had sown weeds in the wheat," and, as a result, many Christians simply had not learned how to pray with each other at home for anything, much less for healing. Many Christians who came to church every Sunday had never learned to pray with each other at home. When I first began to realize this sad situation, I started checking out my impressions by asking groups of Christians at conferences and retreats: "How many of you can remember your father ever praying for your healing when you were sick as a child?" By now, I have asked this simple question of more than a hundred thousand people, and their responses seem to show that only about 3% can remember their fathers praying with them when they were sick.[1] This is extraordinary! It means that about 97% of churchgoing Christians, who presumably come from more fervent Christian homes and have taken the trouble to come and hear us speak, have never had the experience of their fathers praying with them when they were sick. When I ask the same question about mothers, the record is better, and the percentage rises to about 20%. But still, isn't it tragic when four out of every five cannot remember their mothers praying with them? The reason has to be that their parents never thought that the prayer would work—that their sick children might be healed.

Again, when you ask married couples if they pray with one another, you find that the vast majority — if they pray at all — pray only formal prayers, like grace at meals.

This lack of shared family prayer is a terrible personal loss, and it's so common that married couples don't even realize they are missing anything. You seldom hear a sermon about praying together; yet, it seems to me that missing out on shared prayer is a loss as serious as not attending church on Sunday. For instance, many Christians feel distant from God, unsure about whether he loves them. Often this distance goes back to childhood: If my father didn't feel close enough to God to speak to him in my presence, chances are my own religion will be very private, and God will seem remote.

Probably I will resent it when I am asked to change from a quiet Sunday liturgy where everyone leaves me alone to one where I am supposed to sing enthusiastically or give the people around me the kiss of peace. My relationship to God is likely to be very formal and I may find it hard to experience the kind of friendship with Jesus that he himself holds out to me: "I shall no longer call you servants. . . . I call you friends" (Jn 15:15).

If I were a young person thinking about marrying, I would make it a priority to find a partner who would pray with me every day. I can tell a real difference on those rare days when my wife Judith and I are not able to start the day by praying together. Without praying together, it is harder for couples to forgive each other when quarrels and misunderstandings arise. When we do pray together, we have a real sense of the presence of God; something deep within us comes together. I am not exaggerating in saying that these times praying together are the best times of our day.

Again, if I am living in community or with a roommate in college, what a help it is when we can pray together from time to time very simply. Many ministers and priests, whose hearts cry out for a more personal form of prayer life, suffer precisely because other members of their communities want nothing more than formal prayers.

At any rate, praying together at home is such a beautiful experience—and so easy to learn that the present bleak record could easily be changed if people were taught and "given permission" to try. So far as I know, there is no teaching in any Christian church forbidding praying together at home; in fact, quite the contrary. This makes the poor record of actual practice all the more mysterious, unless it comes from the very human problem of priests and ministers concentrating so much on what happens in formal church worship that they neglect teaching families what they can do at home.

Because much of my work has been showing ordinary Christians that God can work extraordinary healings through them, I have long wanted to be able to give friends a short, simple book showing them how to pray for healing.[2] The simplest answer to that was to write a little book myself. So that is what you now have in your hands.

Over the years, many married couples have come to ask for prayer. For instance, a husband might bring his wife who was suffering from cancerous tumors. As we started to pray for the wife, the husband might wander off to a corner of the room as if he did not consider himself expert enough to pray for his own wife. Then we would have to encourage him to join us. For the most part, husbands and wives have not prayed with their sick partner or child even in the privacy of their home. Who knows how much cancer, arthritis and heart disease could be healed if only ordinary Christians learned how to pray with one another? Again and again, we have had to bring husbands and wives out of the corner, as it were, lead them to their partner and say: "You can do it. Jesus wants to use you to bless and even to heal your partner." So many wonderful, loving Christians have just never learned to pray with the simple confidence that their prayers can make a real difference.

It's hard to believe that I wrote *The Prayer That Heals* in 1981—so many years ago. In its first twenty-four years, more than 154,000 copies were sold. But the most satisfying thing to me, of course, is that people have not only read the book but have been encouraged to act on it—to pray for healing for their families and friends. They find it is true, it is real, it works! A recent letter reads:

"While reading *The Prayer That Heals*, God began an inner healing within me. By the

> last chapter, I was in tears as the healing power of Almighty God enveloped me. Past hurts came to light and the healing power of the Holy Spirit took them away. I feel totally freed from those old hurts."

Even if that happened only once, it would have been worth all the time it took to write this book. But it can happen for you, for your family and your friends. I invite you to try it—the prayer that heals. You'll see for yourself

Francis S. MacNutt
October 28, 2004
Jacksonville, Florida

One:
God Still Heals Today

What God would like to do for and through you is so wonderful that you may find it hard to believe! God wants ordinary people like you to bless and heal one another in your families. When you start to pray with others, amazing things will happen to you and to your loved ones. I want to encourage you to believe the truth that many Christians today have never been taught to believe: Jesus will heal his people through your prayers.

If you need encouragement to pray for your sick friends, just take the example of Jesus himself. In the Gospels you see him spending a large part of his time going from one sick person to another, laying his hands on them and healing them. His heart goes out to people — like the time he was tired and tried to get away from the crowd to rest with his disciples.

> But the crowds got to know and they went after him. He made them welcome and talked to them about the kingdom of God; and he cured those who were in need of healing (Lk 9:11).

In short, he was tired of mobs and tried to get away, but when he saw the people, their suffering broke down his resolve. So he talked to them and healed them, even though he was exhausted.

He knew so clearly that a central part of his mission was to go among the suffering, especially the poor, and to heal them. How often we read about Jesus putting his fingers into the ears of a deaf man and saying, "Be opened"; putting mud cakes on the eyes of a blind man and telling him to wash in a pool; or simply saying the words, "Your faith has healed you." The leaders who were interested in discussion (the scribes and Pharisees) had to leave the big city of Jerusalem and try to find him in the hills, in the middle of the crowds who were clustered around him, grasping for healing.

His fame spread throughout Syria, and those who were suffering from diseases and painful complaints of one kind or another, the possessed, epileptics, the paralyzed, were all brought to him, and he cured them (Mt 4:24).

When you consider how much time Jesus spent praying with people, there had to be a reason for it.

The reason was simple: Jesus came to our fallen, wounded humanity to save and free us in every way. His Father—and ours —saw how miserable we were, in what sin, in what sickness, in what pain. Having compassion, he sent his only Son, Jesus, who was like us in every respect (except sin)—someone who understood us and our pain because he himself shared it. But there was one big difference: Because he was the Son of God he had the *power* in himself to change things.

He could forgive sins and heal sickness. "Everyone in the crowd was trying to touch him because power came out of him that cured them all" (Lk 6:19). Whenever sick people reached out to him, he, in turn, reached out to them and their sickness disappeared.

He did all this because his mission was to save us and rescue us from the miserable state we were in: It was the very reason he came. When John the Baptist sent his followers to ask Jesus if he were the Messiah, Jesus simply showed that he was carrying out his saving mission:

> Go back and tell John what you have seen and heard: the blind see again, the lame walk, those suffering from virulent skin-diseases are cleansed, and the deaf hear, the dead are raised to life, the good news is proclaimed to the poor; and blessed is anyone who

does not find me a cause of falling.
(Lk 7:22-23).

Jesus wasn't boasting or trying to prove some point about being divine; he was just carrying out his work, his work as savior of the human race. He loved people. He saw them as his brothers and sisters, and he couldn't stand to see them wounded and hurting, any more that we can stand by and see the people we love suffer needlessly when there is something we can do for them.

He proclaimed the Good News: "The kingdom of God is at hand!" Life, health and love. The kingdom of Satan is being destroyed! Death, sickness and hate.

Can you see how much Jesus loved people? How much his heart went out to the sick? How he spent hours making his way through crowds and touching foul, leprous sores, even when it was against the law of his day to touch lepers? He really did care for us. He even healed on the Sabbath, straightening up a woman who had been bent over for 18 years (Lk 13:10-17), when it meant that the religious leaders would turn on him. One more day wouldn't have been intolerable, but he wasn't about to let her suffer even one more day.

Now, if that was part of his daily schedule, going out into the reeking crowds every day to touch and heal them 2000 years ago, do you think he is any less willing to do it today? At the Last Supper he told his followers that things were going to be better for them after he left, after he died and rose from the dead, because then the Spirit would be sent to empower them to do the same deeds that he himself had done (Jn 14:12)— and even greater deeds. He was going to live on in us and, by the power of the Spirit, would continue to heal in the 20th century as he had in the first.

Some Christians find it hard to believe that Jesus still wants to heal them in extraordinary ways, that healing is meant to be as ordinary, as frequent, as it was when Jesus walked out through the crowds every day in the glaring hot sun of Galilee.

You already know this just by studying the life and words of Jesus, especially in the Gospel of Luke. But you can also see it for yourself if you pray and ask Jesus to heal your friends and members of your family.

Just in the past six weeks alone I have seen five extraordinary cases of feet that were crippled and smaller than the normal foot, grow out and become the same size as the normal foot. In two of the cases the crippling was caused by polio. In one case a woman's foot grew from size 4 to size 7 as we prayed. I mention these because clearly the problem was not psychosomatic; a real bone growth had to take place for the changes to take place. In one instance, it took only 10 minutes; in another it took two hours.

But what a wonderful thing: to see God's healing power at work under our very eyes! I didn't always have so much belief in the willingness of Jesus to answer my prayers, but I have now seen so much it would be hard for me not to believe.

Step one in learning to pray with people is to believe that Jesus is still at work healing his people today. You will see marvelous evidence of this if you just put into practice the few simple things I will suggest in this book.

Know that Jesus loves you and that he has both the desire and the power to heal you. *Believe* it and in time you will *experience* it. Finally, you will *know* it with a certainty that no one can shake: Jesus loves you and wants to heal his beloved people.

Two:
Through You

It was fairly easy for me to believe that God was still willing to heal people in extraordinary ways through prayer. To encourage my faith I used to read eagerly the lives of holy people and the stories of God's wonderful works. It strengthened my faith to hear stories of how God still worked in our day. One book I read with fascination was Dr. Alexis Carrel's *Voyage to Lourdes*. Dr. Carrel was a skeptical physician who wanted to go to Lourdes with a trainload of sick people in order to gather evidence of the Catholic church's cruelty in building up the unrealistic hopes of the sick, crowding them into train cars (this was in the early 1900s) and making them suffer the bouncing of the railroad on a fruitless quest for healing. Once he got on the crowded train he was asked to administer morphine to a woman dying of tuberculosis of the peritoneum. To Dr. Carrel, she represented exactly the kind of suffering patient who should be spared the pain of being carted off to Lourdes, where he judged she would probably die. Lourdes to him was not hope for the sick; instead, it represented cruelty and superstition. The tubercular woman, however, survived the trip, was examined by the doctors of the Medical Bureau, and then was wheeled out for the blessing of the sick. Dr. Carrel stayed close to her to alleviate her suffering with morphine, but also because he expected to watch her die, right there at Lourdes. Then he could write it up in a Paris journal and expose Lourdes for the mockery he saw it to be.

But wonder of wonders, at the blessing of the sick, he saw her distended abdomen flatten right down; he took her pulse and temperature and found them to be normal. Afterward, the doctors at the Medical Bureau checked her and could find no trace of the disease.

Dr. Carrel was honest enough to write up his account, the reverse of what he had originally intended. Yet, because he was afraid of what his medical colleagues would think, he signed his little book "Dr. Lerrac" (Carrel spelled backward), so that no one but his friends would guess that he wrote it.

I used to devour that kind of book because it encouraged me in my faith. The problem was that I seldom saw anything like that myself; it always seemed to occur in a far-off place like France. Like so many Christians—Catholic, Orthodox and Protestant—I didn't expect Jesus to work such wonders through me. Maybe someone who was holy could pray and the sick might be healed, but I had no right to expect much to happen when I prayed. I believed in healing, but not *through me*: "Lord, I am not worthy."

Is this true of you? If your husband is sick, do you believe that God could heal him through your prayer? If your daughter is sick, would you have any confidence that you might lay your hands on her and see her restored to health?

Part of the Good News is that God wants to use your words and the touch of your hands to heal your loved ones. Even if you do not feel worthy or holy, Jesus wants to use you to pray for the needs in your family and your community.

The entire New Testament shows Jesus trying to *share* his powers with his followers. When Jesus looked at the crowds and had compassion on them because they were like sheep without a shepherd (Mt 9:36-38), he prayed that the Lord of the Harvest would send other laborers to reap the harvest. Even though he was the Son of God he did not want to do it alone; he needed help. Because his work included healing, he shared his healing power with human beings. He didn't reserve it to himself. His instructions to them were:

Cure the sick, raise the dead, cleanse those suffering from virulent skin-diseases, drive out devils. (Mt 10:8)

Later, when the twelve were no longer a large enough band to go to all the cities and villages, he chose others and shared with them the very same powers (Lk 10:1-12). We know that the twelve were very specially chosen as apostles, the foundations of the church, forerunners of the bishops and leaders to come in future ages, but the seventy-two seem to have been appointed just for the task and they later disappeared from view—reminiscent of the seventy-two elders appointed to help Moses when he was over-burdened (Nm 11:11ff.). The seventy-two who are nameless seem to stand for ordinary people like us.

Later, when the Spirit descended upon all Christians at Pentecost, it was to empower the *entire* Christian community to perform the works that Jesus did: "These are the signs that will be associated with believers: . . . they will lay their hands on the sick who will recover" (Mk 16:17-18).

Do you see how clear the progression is?

1) Jesus comes, sent by the Father, empowered to free and heal his people. He alone is our savior.

2) He shares his mission and his power with the twelve.

3) The needs of the people are overwhelming. So, he shares his mission and power with the seventy-two.

4) At Pentecost, he shares that mission and that power of the Spirit with *all the people* (although aspects of leadership and authority are reserved for Peter and the twelve). This sharing includes the generations that are to come.

That includes *you*. You, who are reading this right now, are empowered by Jesus to pray for people, to heal the sick. The main condition is that you be Christian, although it is also important that you have received the empowering of the Spirit through confirmation or the baptism of the Spirit.[1] If you launch out, God will use you even now as you pray with your family and friends—and the larger world as well.

It is so important for you to know that Jesus needs *your* prayers, in spite of your weakness. You are not being proud or making yourself out as someone special if you start to pray for the sick; you are just acting as a normal Christian should.

When I first began to pray with people, a sense of spiritual inferiority was my main problem, too. I felt as if I were putting on an act, especially since no one else that I was closely associated with was praying with people. I was afraid of looking ridiculous or being labeled as overly pious. It may be that way with you, too. You are going to have to get over your fear of seeming different. I find that even husbands and wives are hesitant to pray with each other.

All these fears have robbed us of what Jesus bequeathed to all his followers. How otherwise can we explain why most Christian fathers and mothers seldom pray with their children?

But when you finally do get the courage to pray — simply in obedience to God's word, if for no other reason — you will discover in a real way that Jesus hears your prayers. You will never want to turn back. If you have never done this, have never prayed with someone before, you may resist what I am saying here. But once you have prayed several times and seen how wonderfully Jesus answers you, you will regret all the years you have missed praying with your friends. You will be like the seventy-two who came back rejoicing because they had seen the marvelous results of their prayer: " 'Lord,' they said, 'even the devils submit to us when we use your name' " (Lk 10:17).

No matter how weak you may feel as a Christian, no matter how lacking in the ability to create a beautiful prayer, it makes no difference. God hears the prayers of the little ones. "But we hold this treasure in pots of earthenware, so that the immensity of the power is God's and not our own" (2 Cor 4:7). Unworthiness is common to us all. All that counts is Jesus telling us to have confidence: "Ask and you shall receive." But moving from the realization of truth to actually starting to pray with people is so difficult. You are afraid of launching out, of seeming different, so you hold back. How can you get started?

All I know is that I had to start one day in a simple way. I just began to ask people, "Would you like me to pray with you about that?" To my surprise, they almost all said, "Yes." Even the skeptics said: "I've got nothing to lose. If you believe that God can help, go ahead." I try to present the invitation in a simple, quiet way, so that people won't feel pushed into something. I ask in such a way that they can easily say, "No," if they don't want me to pray. But almost always they say, "Yes."

Asking the people closest to you to pray —your husband or your wife, for instance— is often the hardest because their "No" would be a painful rejection. But that's part of the life of a Christian, and we will never begin unless we ask. We receive from God if we ask, and we can only receive from our fellow human beings, if we ask.

The reward is so great! It's not just that prayers are answered—as they are. It's also that I seldom feel my love for other people as deeply, in a real, non-possessive way, as when I pray for them and see them change right before me. And I seldom experience the love others have for me as much as when I break down, confess my own weakness and admit to my friends that I need their prayers.

On the days when I don't pray with my wife for the life I need that day, something is really missing. I experience an aching vacuum. This is not something I have been taught; it is just a reality. I need the prayers of the people closest to me to survive, just as I need some time of solitary prayer. It's like the emptiness many people feel when they are used to receiving the Lord in the Eucharist and then, some morning, they miss receiving. So it is with the joined prayer of loved ones. If you haven't experienced it, you can't realize what you are missing. Even Jesus seemed to need it; what else explains the disappointment he felt in Gethsemane when he came back, after his solitary agony, to his three closest friends and found them asleep?

I find that even in those Christian groups that believe in prayer for healing, there is a tendency to depend too much on the celebrity healer and the big healing service. I think it is a wonderful thing to have healing services, but not at the expense of praying at home for the sick. Just recently I had a chance to check with a group of 600 people the day after they took part in a healing service where many were prayed for. Of the 600, six said they were totally healed and another 25 were improved. Now, it was wonderful that about 1% were totally healed and another 4% were improved, but I believe that about 75% could be totally healed or improved if we could spend the time praying in small groups of friends. I was once part of a small group that met every Wednesday night and prayed for two hours for the sick; *most* of the sick were visibly changed each week when we prayed.

Occasionally someone we pray for is totally healed, but mostly it's gradual—like Marianne, a nine-year-old girl who was profoundly retarded and whose body didn't move properly as a result of an overdose of flu vaccine, administered when she was three. Five times, she went to the prayer sessions and three of those five times her parents observed a change, either then or in the following week. Finally, she was able to lift her leg and take her first step since the overdose. A feeble step,

certainly, with Marianne being held up and sup-
ported by her father, but it was a step, the first in
six years. As she took it, the group gathered
around and applauded; we were so happy to see
hope reborn in her parents as they saw the Lord at
work in their daughter.

The same thing can happen as you learn the
truth that will set you free: Jesus wants to use *your*
prayers to bless and heal people. You don't have to
be special—just an ordinary Christian, aware of
your own weakness, or what you consider your
own lack of faith.

Jesus wants to heal *through you.*

He will if you just give him the chance.

Three:
Praying With People

Once you discover that God really answers you when *you* pray, the next step is for you to learn to pray *with* people, as well as *for* them, at a distance. For many years, I prayed for people at a distance: A name would go up on the bulletin board, and later I would pray when I was alone in church or in my office. That is a good way of praying. I still pray that way often, especially after someone has written a letter, asking for prayer; after all, Jesus cured the centurion's servant at a distance without bothering to travel to his home.

But when a friend asks you for prayer face to face, the most natural thing is to pray right then and there, on the spot. It used to be that when someone would ask me to pray, I would make a promise, "I'll remember you in my prayers," but I never thought of stopping to pray with him. No one had ever directly discouraged me from praying with people, yet, strange as it may seem, it never crossed my mind to do so. To me prayer was a private thing, except for the public prayers of the church. I would have been embarrassed to make up a prayer for someone; talking to God was too personal a thing to do with someone listening to me.

The strange thing is that, although there is no teaching that I know of in any church that would discourage Christians from praying spontaneously with one another, most Christians from mainline churches simply do not pray with each other in their own words. This is a special loss when we find that families do not feel comfortable praying together. Nor do priests or ministers, by and large (with the exception of grace at meals), pray with each other in their own words.[1]

Some of our reluctance to pray probably goes back to our fear of revealing our inmost thoughts and feelings to one another. I remember vividly one meeting of theologians in Rome in 1975. Father Kilian McDonnell, O.S.B., shared with this distinguished group that he once thought the charismatic renewal was not for him personally because it was overly emotional, even though it was a great help to many people. Later, he continued, he came to realize that that was simply a pitiful excuse. The real reason he had difficulty was that the renewal was *too personal.*

I think that is the trouble with most of us in the beginning: We are locked up inside ourselves and prefer to be formal and impersonal in our religious observances. We are *afraid* to pray out loud in somebody's presence. I, for one, was certainly afraid of being ridiculed for appearing pious. Several times my father indicated to me that he would like me to pray for his health, but I could not bring myself to do it until near his death in the hospital's intensive care unit. Just thinking of it I could feel myself blush with embarrassment.

The block was not on his part: he was a gentle man, who really wanted me to pray with him.

So, we need to be set free, to be given permission to pray with each other. When I am talking to a room full of people I can suggest that they try praying with one another right then and there and get over that initial fear. But since you are probably reading this book alone, all I can do is encourage you to pray with the people closest to you whenever the next natural opportunity comes up—for instance, when your child is sick, pray with the child and ask your husband or wife to join you.

What advantage is there in praying with someone when the Lord can help people at a distance? Well, there does seem to be an additional *power* that is there—I can tell you that from experience. Perhaps it's because the person you are praying with can hear your prayer, and that builds up his or her faith. Perhaps it's the touch of your hand through which the power of God flows in a tangible way. Also, there seems to be a special presence of God when several people are gathered together in love:

> In truth I tell you once again, if two of you on earth agree to ask anything at all, it will be granted to you by my Father in heaven. For where two or three meet in my name, I am there among them. (Mt 18:19-20)

Most of the instantaneous, dramatic healings I have seen take place have been when there was a large gathering of Christian people, all praising God. God really does seem to dwell in the praises of his people, so I prefer to pray together with someone else, whenever possible. I have not only gotten over most of my fear, but now I prefer praying with people, so that we can see what's happening and as we talk with the person to find out how best to pray.

Most of all, when we pray with one another, we sense the love of Jesus, the sure sign of his presence. Once I was asked to pray for a 60-year-old Catholic sister who was going to the hospital the next day for an operation on the brain. At that time her community members were not familiar with praying for healing spontaneously as a group, but they gathered around to join me in praying. As we finished, her face was radiant and streaked with tears, as she said, "I have never before experienced the love of my community as deeply as I have tonight."

My prayer for you is that, as you pray with your loved ones, you come to know the love and the healing power of Jesus more deeply than ever before.

Four:
Touch

Once you learn to pray *with* your friends, you will begin to understand why the Gospels lay such great stress upon touching people when you pray—the laying on of hands. "These are the signs that will be associated with believers: . . . they will lay their hands on the sick, who will recover" (Mk 16:17-18). If I had been Mark, writing that section of the Gospel, I would probably have written "they will pray for the sick," rather than "they will lay their hands on the sick," but Mark and the other disciples realized that, even without words, there is a healing power in just touching another person. A mother demonstrates this when she picks up her crying child and holds it close and kisses away the hurt. She knows intuitively that her holding the child comforts and soothes it.

But, deeper than that, when you touch as well as pray for the other person, something else happens. In addition to the soothing, a *power* or gentle current often goes out from your hand to assist in the healing. Jesus was well aware of this. Once when he was in a crowd, a woman suffering from an issue of blood decided that if she could just touch his clothes she would be healed. So she sneaked around in the crowd until she could touch him, and instantly the bleeding stopped. (She was doing all this secretively because, according to the law, a woman bleeding in this way was ritually unclean, and she was afraid Jesus wouldn't break the law and touch her.) But Jesus, knowing he had been touched, looked around in the crowd and said, "Who touched my clothes?" He was aware that *"power had gone out from him"* (Mk 5:25-34).

Another time St. Luke recounts that "Everyone in the crowd was trying to touch him because power came out of him that cured them all" (Lk

6:19). It wasn't only Jesus who seemed to emanate this kind of life-giving power. His followers did, too. The people used to lay their sick out in the streets hoping that Peter's shadow might fall across them (Acts 5:15), and others would take handkerchiefs that Paul had touched and use them for healing the sick and casting out evil spirits (Acts 19:11-12).

In short, the early Christians had a lively sense of healing and the power of touch. Since you don't have the spiritual stature of St. Peter or St. Paul, you may think it prideful to claim to have some significant spiritual power in your hands. I know, because I certainly felt that way myself when I first began to pray *with* people instead of just *for* them. But remember, the Gospel of Mark (16:17) says that one of the signs that will follow *believers*, not just holy people, is that they will lay their hands on the sick who will recover.

As a Christian, you also know that the Father, the Son and the Holy Spirit dwell within you. This is a traditional belief of Christians, taken from the last discourse of Jesus in St. John (chapters 14-17). The life of the Trinity is within you; that life of God within you (sanctifying grace in Catholic terminology) is a gift and no credit on your part, but it should have an effect on other people if you let it burn brightly.

Nearly every day I see this communication of life from one person to another take place. When we lay our hands upon sick people, they almost always experience *heat*. It's not an ordinary heat that just touches the surface of the skin but a warmth that seems to search deep into whatever organ has been affected by sickness. (Occasionally, the reverse happens: Persons suffering from overheating in the joints due to arthritis experience coolness when we lay hands upon their knees or fingers.) Furthermore, I, for one, have a low body temperature, so my skin temperature is usually cooler than that of the person I am praying for (especially if he or she has a fever). It seems as if the heat is caused by the sick person's body, by its response to being stimulated by God's power. Try to see, by the eye of your faith, the life of God within you— the life of the Father, Son and Holy Spirit. It really is light and life, so strong in you that it can radiate light and life to every-one around you. If you believe the common teaching of Christianity—that God lives within you—you should find it easy to see that your touch can heal! That doesn't make you an extraordinary Christian, a saint. It just means that you are an ordinary Christian. This is in itself extraordinary!

In fact, I know several people who were healed just by being looked at. They experienced the presence of Jesus coming through a Christian's eyes, and it was enough to heal them. Nor should this surprise us. If we can be infected with sickness by getting near sick people, why shouldn't we be touched by life and health when we draw close to the source of life, Jesus?

So, if you have never prayed with someone and put your hand upon them while you prayed, I encourage you to try it. If your child is sick, laying your hand upon the child is such a natural thing to do anyway. It should be just as natural to pray for a husband, wife or friend—once you get over that initial shyness. Holding a person's hand or putting your arm around a shoulder is such a natural gesture. If the person is sick and it can be done decently, put your hand near the affected area while you are praying.

If you do start praying with people, you should soon see enough healings take place through your touch to encourage you and strengthen your faith even more.

For instance, you may pray with a person who has a tumor and, as you put your hand upon that tumor, you may gradually see it disappear. At first, you won't be sure: Is it just your imagination? But then, as you pray, you find, to your amazement, that it really is shrinking. Usually, it just takes one or two experiences like that to convince you that God still wants ordinary people like you—simple believers—to lay hands upon the sick who will then recover.

There is one beautiful discovery about healing touch that I would especially like to share, and that is how wonderful it is for a husband (or friends) to pray for a pregnant wife and her unborn baby.[1] Sometimes the baby gives its first kick as the mother is prayed for—life responding to life. Of course, if the mother is alone she can put her hand upon her stomach and pray for the child. A mother can actually play with her unborn child by placing her hand, first on one side, then on the other. The baby will turn in the womb, gradually shifting around until its back is toward the mother's loving hand. Parents who have prayed for their children before birth report that these children seem to be happier, cry less and have better dispositions than their children born in previous years without such prayer. It's something like John the Baptist responding in Elizabeth's womb when Mary, bearing Jesus, came to visit: "Now it happened that as soon as Elizabeth heard Mary's greeting, the child leaped in her womb and Elizabeth was filled with the Holy Spirit" (Lk 1:41). This biblical scene reminds me of a healing seminar in Tulsa when we prayed with a pregnant mother: At that very moment, she felt her child leap as she herself was filled with the Spirit! What could be a more beautiful and natural scene than a husband and wife praying together for their unborn child!

Five:
In Your Own Words

For many years, I was hesitant about making up a prayer in my own words; no one had ever encouraged me to do so. The prayers I said were memorized prayers like the "Our Father." Certainly it is good to memorize prayers as a child and use them as an adult. But, we have many specific needs that can best be voiced by specific prayer.

Jesus and his disciples felt free to make up prayers that suited the need of the moment. So far as I know neither Jesus nor his followers repeated the same prayer twice when praying with people;

they simply spoke to God as we speak to one another. Prayer is a heart-to-heart conversation with God who loves us. In our ordinary conversation with friends we don't write speeches or repeat what was said last time. Even the "Our Father" does not seem to have been memorized word for word by the early Christian communities, for Matthew and Luke have different versions of it. The version we memorize is from Matthew (6:9-13), but Luke's version is much shorter:

> Father, may your name be
> held holy,
> your kingdom come;
> give us each day our daily bread,
> and forgive us our sins,
> for we ourselves forgive each one
> who is in
> debt to us.
> And do not put us to the test
> (Lk 11:2-4)

Luke, then, seems concerned about the main drift of the Lord's prayer and not about a word-for-word memorization.

The apostles, too, were free in making up their own prayers to suit the person they were praying with. For instance, Peter said to a paralytic: "Aeneas, Jesus Christ cures you: get up and make your bed" (Acts 9:34). To the lame man at the Gate Beautiful, Peter said, "I have neither silver nor gold, but I will give you what I have: in the name of Jesus Christ the Nazarene, walk!" (Acts 3:6).

I could give countless other examples; the point is simply that the followers of Jesus felt free to make up prayers to suit the needs of the people they were praying with. On the other hand, many Christians from mainline churches have become so used to formal, memorized prayers that they are afraid of launching out and becoming personal about their faith in public.[1] Perhaps the fear is of appearing pious. Perhaps it is the fear of making a mistake in a church group where doctrine has been emphasized. In any case, many Christians seldom voice a personal prayer, except for an occasional grace at meals.

Yet, no church teaches against voicing your own prayer, and it is a most natural thing to do—a Christian heritage of which our fears have robbed us. When you do pray from the heart in your own words it is a most beautiful thing. I remember one of the first times I ever heard someone pray in his own words. It was during the first "cursillo" held in Iowa in the early 1960s. One night a few of us had gone into the chapel and a burly truck driver began praying to Jesus in his own words about the mess he felt he had made of his life, and all of us in the room began to weep. For years we had all said this kind of prayer privately, but to hear an ordinary person, a truck driver, open up his heart was something I had never heard before. So there I was, more than 30 years old, hearing a spontaneous prayer for the first time.

Aside from getting rid of our fears, making up a prayer should be easy. It's as easy as talking to someone who is our friend, for Jesus has assured us that we are his friends. He has encouraged us over and over to ask his Father for anything, according to his will, and it will be granted.

Our fearlessness towards him consists in this,

that if we ask anything in accordance with his will he hears us.

And if we know that he listens to whatever we ask him,

we know that we already possess whatever we have asked of him. (1 John 5:14-15)

He told us not to babble or make up long prayers—all we need to do is voice a simple prayer from the heart.

There are several ways that you can pray for healing. For instance, some Christians who are specially close to Jesus and who can sense when he wants to heal a particular person, can say a prayer of *command*, just as Jesus commanded the waves and wind to die down and Peter commanded the lame man to walk. Since the kingdom of God involves restoring everything to its proper order, the Christian may be given the authority to pray the prayer of command. The forces of nature, then, must obey when this prayer is backed by the authority of God. At times, for example, I pray a prayer of command for cancer patients: "In the name of Jesus Christ I command these cancer cells to wither up and die. I command these tumors to shrink up and dissolve. From now on let nothing but normal cells be reproduced in this body. In the name of Jesus I command this cancer to leave this body that it may be whole."

Now to say that kind of prayer of command demands that you have a sure sense of what God wants, and it may sound beyond the confidence that most of us can muster when we are learning to pray.

What you can easily do, though, is simply to *ask* God for what you want: "Jesus, please send your healing power into my wife's body and kill the cancer cells. Dissolve the tumors and fill her with new strength. Give the command that normal, healthy cells be produced by her body from now on. Lord, please heal my wife and restore her to our family." That kind of prayer should be easy to make up—simply speak to God what is in your heart, with no pretense. You know he loves you, so just talk to him as a friend.

Somehow we have the idea that we have to make up an elaborate prayer to impress God, that if our prayer is ordinary God won't hear it. But that's not true. You don't have to pray in King James English; just speak the way you would to a friend. Nor do you have to pray in some tone of voice different from the tone you would use speaking to a friend at dinner. Be yourself when you pray—with no artificiality. "In your prayers do not babble as the gentiles do, for they think that by using many words they will make themselves heard" (Mt 6:7).

Your prayer in English need not be more than a few minutes long. If you are accustomed to praying in tongues that can be a help, too. The way I usually pray is to pray in English for a little bit and then pray in tongues for as long as I feel it's helpful while keeping my hand upon the person's shoulder or other affected part. By praying in tongues I am turning the prayer over to the Holy

Spirit who understands, far better than I, what is best to pray for. The prayer, then, rises above the limitations of my understanding of the situation. On several occasions while I was praying in tongues, the person I was praying with heard me praying in a language he or she understood and I didn't (in one instance, Arabic: in another, Greek). They all found the experience very helpful—and encouraging (in two of the instances the persons were not charismatic and were skeptical about tongues previous to this prayer).

But I don't want to belabor the benefit of praying in tongues. You can pray in English—or whatever your native language is—in the most simple, natural way, and the Lord will respond to your prayer.

"Ask, and it will be given to you; search, and you will find; knock, and the door will be opened to you" (Lk 11:9).

Six:
It Takes Time

One of the greatest discoveries in my prayer life has been that when a short prayer doesn't seem to help, a "soaking" prayer often brings the healing we are looking for. Over and over I have checked the effect of prayer by asking groups how many were *totally healed* when we prayed a short prayer and how many were *improved*. The number of people who experience some real improvement usually outnumbers those who are totally healed by about twenty-five to one. This led me to realize that a short prayer usually has some physical effect (and always a spiritual effect) upon a person, but that most of us need to take more time when we pray for the sick.

One night, I prayed with about fifteen people and two or three seemed completely healed. But, the majority experienced improvement. The longer we prayed, the better they felt. One was a secretary whose fingers were tightening up with arthritis, a frightening prospect, since it could mean the loss of her job. The week before, when we prayed, about half the stiffness left. Last night, to her great delight, it almost disappeared! The time element seems to be essential; the straightening of her fingers took two sessions of prayer. Other times it takes much longer.

Many healings could take place in your family prayer if you simply would spend time with one another, praying in the simple ways I have mentioned. Suppose your elderly father has arthritis, especially in the spine and fingers. If you pray with him in your own words and simply ask Jesus—or the Father—to heal him, and then hold his fingers in your hands or put your hand upon his back and continue to pray in silence,[1] or pray in tongues, or sing gently (whatever seems right to you), you may very well see a change take place before your eyes. This usually takes place in stages, so the following are things to look for:

First, the *pain* will diminish and, perhaps, completely go away in the course of about 10 minutes (sometimes more, sometimes less).

Next, look for a return of *mobility* and flexibility. Ask him to move his fingers, or bend his spine and see if it is more flexible. This usually takes longer.

Last, if he has *swellings* on the joints you may see the swelling go down and the gnarled fingers start to straighten. (When I pray, this usually becomes visible in about half an hour.)

I want to encourage you by letting you know that these changes start to take place *most of the time* when we pray with arthritis patients. While I realize that God may have given me (and many others) a special gift in praying for healing, still I believe that similar blessings will happen in your family if you pray. It may take a little longer, perhaps, but healing will often come while you pray. What I say here of arthritis you can apply to praying for other physical sicknesses.

At times, I have had to pray for hours with one person until the healing was complete. You will find that it is work, but it is worth every moment, for it is such a delight to be able to bring God's healing to someone. Another person we prayed with last night, a young woman with scoliosis, was so happy, her face covered with tears of joy, because she could feel her spine straightening and the pain leaving while the prayer was going on.

There are different ways of spending time praying with someone. Sometimes I feel drawn to pray an hour or two with someone, with five-minute breaks at regular intervals to rest and check to see if any improvement has taken place.

I usually spend a longer time when there is no chance of seeing the person for some time, or when it is a very serious illness and it's important that healing start as soon as possible. Sometimes so much change and healing is going on that it would be a pity to stop.

In other cases, it seems best just to pray for five minutes a day. This might be specially suitable for a husband and his wife praying with each other for any needs they may have. In any event, having someone pray with you is such a beautiful, strengthening experience that you probably won't want the person or group members to stop praying with you once they have started. The one doing the praying, on the other hand, may have to stop, because prayer usually takes something out of you. (About two hours' praying with people at a healing service is my limit; after that I start to become exhausted.)

As I understand it, the time element of soaking prayer is needed because so much healing comes through *touch*. The longer the sick area is held in the healing light of God, the more the germs or tumors have to wither up and die. I like to think of it as God's radiation treatment. The life of God is transmitted through your hand, but it is not God's undiminished life and power. It is his power all right, but it is filtered through your weakness and your brokenness. So, naturally, it takes time for it to take effect.

For families who have retarded children, or children with cerebral palsy, or who have any kind of serious, chronic sicknesses, soaking prayer is a wonderful help. The instances that I personally know of mental retardation or brain damage being cured have all been through long-term prayer (frequent prayer over a period of years). The family really prayed with the child as a daily commitment. One of the beautiful effects is that the sick person almost always experiences God's love during the prayer, and this in itself is healing. You should also be aware that, with brain damage or ailments with nerve damage where the repair is beyond the power of nature; then a real creative miracle by God is needed, rather than just an ordinary healing. This kind of miracle occurs more rarely than ordinary healing. Occasionally it occurs instantly (often at a large healing service where there is a special presence of God). But when it happens in other settings, it usually takes place over a long period of time where a family is dedicated to praying for that healing.

Right now, for instance, our prayer group prays once a week with a profoundly retarded eight-year-old girl. Her parents also are praying with her every day. After two months of prayer with our group, she is still retarded, but every other week she improves in some tangible way. After last week's prayer, for instance, her eyes started to follow her parents' hand movements, something she had not been able to do before. We see steady progress that her therapists can verify; it seems to be taking place at a much faster pace than natural causes can account for—and yet the healing may take years.

But these gradual healings that take time are such a great sign of hope. When I see a sick person now, my thought is, "If only someone could pray with that cripple in the wheelchair for several hours, I believe she could walk." I hope you recognize the wonderful ability you have to transmit the life of Jesus to the people around you, how you can pray with your friends (or sometimes, strangers) and see their sickness swallowed up in life.

Even Jesus touched a blind man twice before he could see clearly (Mk 8:22-26), and he told us about "the need to pray continually and never lose heart" (Lk 18:1). So be encouraged if you have a loved one who is seriously ill; spend time with that person, pray frequently; lay your hands upon the person for five or more minutes and see if any change takes place. If change does take place, then be encouraged to pray longer, for as long or as often as you both have strength.

If you begin to do this, if you are willing to get down to the work of praying and not settle for the "cheap grace" of an instant prayer, you will begin to see wonders take place as your loved ones grow in wisdom and grace and health.

Seven:
Forgiveness

"Yes, if you forgive others their failings, your heavenly Father will forgive you yours; but if you do not forgive others, your Father will not forgive your failings either" (Mt 6:14-15). Similarly, just as our Father will not forgive us, he will not heal us until we forgive those who have injured us.

Part of this is a natural spiritual law: We have all sinned and, as a sign that we believe God will forgive us out of his compassion and goodness, we must be willing to pass that forgiveness on to others and break the chain of hate that affects the whole human race. "It is someone who is forgiven little who shows little love" (Lk 7:47). We cannot receive the love of Jesus, the lifeblood that circulates through us and keeps us going, unless we are willing to pass it on to others. We need to change our hearts of stone into hearts of flesh.

The tragedy is that so many marriages and other relationships are poisoned and wounded. A mother says something unkind to her child, "It's too bad you are not as pretty as your sister," and 30 years later you may still find that insult rankling in an adult woman who is unsure about herself and finds it hard to trust. She felt betrayed by her mother, the one who was closest to her and knew her best, and the experience has affected her whole life. Or a husband may say something cutting to his wife who retorts in kind. Before you know it, there is a distance between them that tends to widen unless they forgive one another. "Bear with one another; forgive each other if one of you has a complaint against another" (Col 3:13).

So, a vital part of our prayer with one another is talking out any differences that we may have and

expressing our feelings in a constructive way.[1]
Then forgive one another and pray for each other
for any wound you may have inflicted. If you
haven't already discovered it, you will find that
you cannot pray in any real, spontaneous way
with others when you hold something against
them or believe that they have something against
you.

> So then, if you are bringing
> your offering to the altar and
> there remember that your brother
> has something against you, leave
> your offering there before the altar,
> go and be reconciled with your
> brother first, and then come back
> and present your offering. (Mt
> 5:23-24)

Over and over again, I have seen people physically healed once they were willing to forgive
someone who had hurt them! It's amazing how we
Christians are sensitive to such sins as drunken-
ness and adultery, but seem so insensitive to the
hatred we may be constantly nourishing in our

hearts. Usually, we believe that the other person is really bad—or, at least, the person's action is—and he or she doesn't deserve anything but scorn and punishment. When I wrote this book, for instance, Iran was holding 53 hostages from the United States, and everywhere I went, I saw bumper stickers insulting Iran and store signs that said: "Iranians not welcome." A quarter-century later, the hatred shifted to Iraq. Clearly, the destruction of the twin towers of the World Trade Center on 9/11 was a dreadful crime. But, some Christians don't have any compunctions about hating a whole group of the world's people. Hating at a distance is dangerous, but holding grudges at home is more immediately devastating. It not only binds up the person we hate, but it can also bind us up and make us sick. When we hate or harbor anger, without working it out, we hurt ourselves even more than the other person. Our hate may eventually destroy us.

More and more, doctors are discovering the role that unresolved feelings play in making us sick. Dr. and Mrs. Carl Simonton in *Getting Well Again* (Bantam Books, Inc.) found evidence that unresolved loss or trauma can lead to cancer's onslaught; Dr. James Lynch in *The Broken Heart* (Harper & Row, Publishers, Inc.) discovered that a lack of love and community increases the incidence of heart disease; and nearly everyone recognizes that tension and anger building up over a period of time can lead to certain kinds of arthritis and ulcers.

Increasingly, then, physicians and groups that pray for the sick are coming to the same conclusion: Sickness may be caused or aggravated by unresolved emotions, especially fear and anger. Ultimately, we need to forgive, to give up the grudges and resentments that cause adrenaline and other endocrine secretions to continuously pour into our bodily systems, when these hormones were only meant to be secreted by our bodies occasionally to help us during times of emergency. If I am afraid over a long period of time, my shoulders hunch up in a fear reaction; if I am habitually afraid, I may end up with a permanent stoop and my posture will be permanently affected.

How much I need God's help to forgive, especially my enemies! I truly believe that holding grudges is such a natural process that only Jesus can free us.[2] Often I have prayed with someone who was unable to forgive and have asked Jesus to fill the person with his own understanding and love for the other party and then to pour out his forgiving love into the heart of the person who is having a hard time forgiving. Over and over I have seen this prayer answered with the forgiveness that Jesus won upon the cross when he cried out, "Father, forgive them; they do not know what they are doing" (Lk 23:34).

At times, the person you cannot forgive may be yourself. You may feel so guilty that you do not even want to be healed. You are punishing yourself. If this is true for you, it is important that you repent and confess any sin that has not yet been brought to the light. (Those churches that offer sacramental confession give a wonderful opportunity for people to bring their guilt out of the dark and into the light.)

Many people can't *feel* forgiven, even when they *know* they are forgiven. For instance, a woman who has had an abortion may be unable to shake the feeling of guilt, even after repenting, for she knows that her child would be alive if she had not ended his life. That death doesn't change after repentance; something happened to that child and it cannot be changed. When something like this happens, the following approach to prayer is often helpful.

First, have the person imagine Jesus (or the Father) with the eyes of their spirit. (If you are praying alone, you can do this yourself.) Try to see Jesus as clearly as possible and speak to him. Listen to him, should he choose to speak. Or perhaps he will shake your hand or even embrace you. After you have welcomed Jesus in this way and are comfortable, imagine him standing by your side. The door opens and the person with whom you need to be reconciled walks in. Try to see the person clearly with the eyes of your spirit: the expression on the face, the way the hair looks, the look in the eyes. Then, asking Jesus to help you, go up to that person and say or do whatever

Jesus inspires you to do. Often this prayer comes alive in the Spirit. You really seem to see Jesus; he helps you by putting a true desire in your heart to be reconciled. You may end up asking for forgiveness or the other person may ask for yours; you may end up shaking hands or embracing; you may see Jesus with his arms around both of you; you may feel a great weight of resentment being lifted, almost physically, off your shoulders.

You can pray this kind of prayer, too, for a friend. I know of extraordinary things Jesus has done in freeing people of unforgiveness and guilt. For instance, I mentioned earlier that there is often need for a woman to forgive herself if she has undergone an abortion. She also needs to ask forgiveness for her action from the child she has aborted. Although the child is physically dead, the spirit lives on and somewhere in God's universe, that child still exists.

Once I prayed for a woman who wanted to be released from her feeling of guilt. She had gone to confession and asked God's forgiveness, but she still felt guilty. First, I suggested that she ask God to bring her the child, so that she might ask the child's forgiveness for ending its life. After I prayed for that, she was silent for a long time and then she laughed. What she saw was this: God the Father appeared to her, holding the child. She was relieved to see that the child was happy. (Amazingly, the child was about two years old— the age the baby would have been if she had not had the abortion.) Then the child turned to her and smiled, and she knew that she was forgiven. Then the Father turned to her and smiled, and she felt, in that instant, the wonder of God's forgiveness. In this way she knew, totally, that God forgave her, her child forgave her, and she was finally able to forgive herself.

In this kind of prayer there is much creativity— creativity on the level of God's inspiration, on the level of the story of the Prodigal Son. So I encourage you to try it if you are burdened by a soured relationship that you know needs healing. Ask someone to pray with you, or pray alone in the way I have suggested.

If you still are in relationship with the other person, you may need to make an effort to work out a reconciliation. Sometimes a third party, such as a marriage counselor, is needed. One suggestion I would make is this: Ask for forgiveness with humility; offer forgiveness with sensitivity. You can say: "I am sorry I have sinned against you. I shouldn't have done it. Forgive me, loose me, free me."

But if you approach someone and say, "I forgive you," it may sound as if you are taking a superior position and saying, "You have sinned against me, but I am generous enough to forgive you." Several times people have told me unexpectedly that they forgave me, and each time it sounded to me as if they were trying to judge me, and let me know what they thought in a rather sneaky way. For example, what would you think if someone came up to you and said: "You have always appeared to me to be proud and insensitive. I don't know if you are or not, but I shouldn't be judging just because you seem haughty to me. So I ask your forgiveness"?

That kind of statement might come as a shock to you, or make you angry. Here you are being asked to forgive a person for something you didn't even know about! If you need to forgive, the safest thing to do is to forgive quietly, in your heart. Say it out loud only when the other person actually asks for forgiveness.

On the other hand, it's actually best to take the initiative when you are guilty and ask for forgiveness. The other person may not give it, but you have done your part to be reconciled.

Sometimes a relationship suffers, not because you did something wrong, but because there is something missing—especially if that something is an expression of love and appreciation. I know that I never was able to express my love for my mother and father adequately until their last days. If I had been able simply to say, "I love you," it would have made them so much happier.

I remember one woman with whom I prayed after she asked for the healing of her relationship with her father. He had never showed her the love and affection she needed as his daughter. She had earlier received several beautiful inner healings, but after this prayer nothing seemed to happen. As she put it, she felt as if she were in a pressure cooker: the healing had not yet happened. It did not, in fact, take place until several days later when she went to visit her father. She let herself into the house and went to the living room where she saw her father as she had always seen him, watching TV, drinking beer, with his feet propped up on a stool. She was standing at the door, wondering whether or not to go in, when she seemed to hear a voice telling her to go to her dad and tell him that she loved him. At first she resisted, believing that he would only laugh at her. But the inner urging persisted until finally she overcame her reluctance, walked up to his chair, knelt down beside him and said, "Dad, I love you." For a few seconds her fears were realized as he kept staring ahead, watching the TV screen. Then he turned toward her, burst into tears and threw his arms around her. As they wept together, the healing of years of hurt took place.

Clearly, God was not satisfied until reconciliation had taken place not only in her heart, but in reality.

You probably know yourself how loving relationships can free you to be the kind of person you want to be, while hateful relationships bind you up. So do what you can to set others free. I now see a deeper meaning in "Whatever you bind on earth shall be bound in heaven; whatever you loose on earth shall be loosed in heaven."

Although Jesus addressed these words to Peter as he gave him authority in his apostolic band, there is a sense in which all of us can bind and loose each other to do the work of the kingdom. It is true: If you do not forgive, you will not be forgiven or healed.

Over and over, I have seen sick people physically healed at the moment they were able to forgive a long-standing enemy. In *Power to Heal* (Ave Maria Press, 1977) I wrote about the healing of Teresa's leg which had been dreadfully warped and twisted by osteomyelitis. On the second day of our prayer the healing seemed to stop. At that point we discovered that Teresa needed to forgive her mother. When Teresa was injured at the age of nine, her mother, who was poor, had to turn her over to a group of sisters who could give Teresa the medical attention she needed. Although her mother was doing what she thought best, it seemed to Teresa that her mother was abandoning her. She grew angry and distant because of what she felt was rejection. When we asked Teresa to forgive her mother—which she did—her leg started straightening and growing once more.

To me, it is such a mystery how tangled, how wounded our relationships can become in our families and in our communities. It is the mystery of sin. But prayer can enable us to forgive each other and to begin again. If you have been wounded, you need to pray for the power that only Jesus can give you: the power to forgive those who have injured you.

Eight:
The Faith to Be Healed

Unless you grew up in a Pentecostal church, you probably belong to a Christian church where the minister and the people do not expect healing through prayer to take place as an everyday event. But then, if you became involved in a charismatic prayer group, you probably experienced a religious shock as you faced a contradictory belief. Unless you absolutely believe you are going o be healed when they pray for you, some Pentecostals and charismatics maintain that you are lacking in faith. There are leaders in some prayer groups I have visited who believe this to be true. They won't be content unless you "lay claim to your healing"—even if you still have the symptoms of sickness after they have prayed.

Now, there are some good Christians who claim to have that absolute faith in healing. They report many healings that take place through their prayers. But if you have been put off by their absolute demands, or if you simply are being honest enough to say that you are somewhat skeptical because you have never seen any healing take place through prayer, I want to encourage you not to lose heart. A number of the people I have prayed with were healed but didn't seem to have much belief at all. Some were not even Christian. I remember a Buddhist monk who somehow got into one of our retreats in Japan. I had a long discussion with him one night at the table. To him, Christ was a great man, but only one among many in whom a spark of the divine resided. But next night, when we were praying for healing, he came forward and he was mightily touched by God. I think Jesus himself touched him to show him that he, Jesus, was not simply one great teacher among many.

Now faith is important, but I find that Jesus, in his compassion, touches people whom most Christians might judge to be unworthy for one reason or another. I remember visiting the famous Catholic healing shrine in Lourdes, France in 1975 and speaking with the doctors at the Medical Bureau. They were discussing the case of a man who had lost a part of a bone during World War II and the bone was restored during a visit to Lourdes. The doctors were ready to certify the cure as miraculous (a rare occurrence now—only once every two or three years do the doctors at Lourdes do this), but the church officials were unwilling to ratify the cure because the man's marital status was irregular. I find, though, that Jesus heals and blesses people today just as he did 2000 years ago, and that he includes some whom we might judge unworthy of his attention.

Now you may believe that you don't have the kind of faith that would enable Jesus to say to you, "Your faith has healed you; go in peace."[1] Perhaps you don't have a strong faith; perhaps you are even skeptical. You are not sure you will be healed of your illness, or that your prayers for someone else are worth very much.

That's all right; you have to start where you are. So, first of all, be honest. If you have just so much faith, God will work with that. I have seen just about as many people healed who were not sure what was going to happen, as those who were sure. To be sure that you are going to be healed requires a special revelation from God: that revelation is given to some, but not to everyone. The big thing is not to fake it. Just work with whatever belief you have. If God chooses to heal you, that will help increase your faith.

Healing does not always come *from* faith. Sometimes it leads *to* faith.

Secondly, our faith is in God, and the fact that he does heal. (In fact, his healing is part of the salvation Jesus came to bring us.) But unless he reveals it to me, my faith does not mean that I have to believe that he will heal me right now, when I pray. The time element of healing depends on a number of factors. Ultimately, of course, in heaven, "He will wipe away all tears from their eyes; there will be no more death, and no more mourning or sadness or pain" (Rv 21:4).

So what I want to encourage you to believe is this: *Ordinarily, God wants to heal his people as soon as possible.* But there are a variety of reasons why people are not healed when we pray, and they don't all reflect badly on the person who is sick.[2] Death, for instance, comes to us all. It is not the ultimate tragedy, but rather an entrance into new life. Agnes Sanford, a pioneer in the healing ministry, believed that her husband, who had suffered a stroke, was kept alive two years longer than necessary by well-meaning friends who kept praying for him and wouldn't let him go when, in God's perfect timing, he was ready to go.

If you have a lively belief in God's goodness and faith—that he is on the side of life and health and that he also has the *power* to bring us healing when everything we have done has failed—then you have the kind of faith that is sufficient to bring about healing. (Even if you don't have that much faith, pray with what you do have, and you will still find that wonderful things happen.) Just pray as honestly as you can, relax and expect to be surprised.

My experience leads me to believe that the kind of person who most often receives healing is someone who is open and receptive to goodness and love and truth. I have seen a kind of bright-eyed look, the look of a child, and when I see it, I usually sense that the person will be healed. Sometimes you see that look of a child in an eighty-year-old woman; sometimes you see it in a college student. Somehow that open kind of person seems to receive healing most often. The person who has a harder time receiving healing is a controlled person who has to think everything through before acting, a person who is filled with explanations and wants you to give them too, a person who has furrows in the brow and a critical spirit. Often such persons are very religious and live exemplary lives, but letting go and receiving love—even from God—is hard for them.

This openness to receive healing seems to have a lot to do with what Jesus said about becoming like a little child if we wish to enter the kingdom of God (Mt 19:13-15). I think there are people who do not know Jesus yet (like the Roman centurion Cornelius in Acts 10), but who have a readiness of heart to trust and believe and, in my experience, they are the ones most often healed. You can see it in their eyes.

So become like a little child. Don't try to figure out too much. Do not strain. Just be obedient and pray with your friends, and you will find that God is much more caring than you thought he was!

Is there anyone among you who would hand his son a stone when he asked for bread? Or would hand him a snake when he asked for a fish? If you, then, evil as you are, know how to give your children what is good, how much more will your Father in heaven give good things to those who ask him! (Mt 7:9-11)

Nine:
The Love That Heals

The great healing evangelists who have special gifts usually emphasize the kind of *faith* that heals. Their gifts, such as knowing when people are being healed and encouraging them to "claim their healing," may intimidate ordinary people. You may think you have to imitate them or you may just give up and say to yourself, "I don't have that kind of faith, so there's no point in my praying." Or perhaps you are tempted to think that those evangelists are overly emotional and that they are making extravagant claims.

But you, as an ordinary person, don't have to pray like that. As I said in the last chapter, your faith can simply be in God's goodness. He loves this person you are praying for more than you do. What he wants is best, and that probably means he wants to heal him. He loves you enough to listen to your prayers and to answer them. So stress love in praying with members of your family and you can't go wrong.

Several things happen if you pray and concentrate on God's love for you and for your family and friends. First, if you become a non-judgmental loving person, many of your own sicknesses will be taken care of and you will be healthier. More and more doctors are discovering the relationship between our inner spiritual state and the health of our bodies. For instance, some doctors now say that the basic source of heart attack is a distortion of spiritual values that causes us to be too competitive, to value work more than people and to race the clock. That kind of behavior, Type A behavior,[1] sets us up for an early heart attack. I myself am a Type A person, and gradually I am learning to love people more than my work and more than any Christian ministry I might have.

Second, if you sense the love of God for you and the person you pray for, you will be gentle. You can relax ("Why are you so anxious, O you of little faith?"); you can speak in a quiet voice and your prayers will be gentle. You won't need to imitate those who speak in powerful voices or who shout and strain. You can speak to God in the same tone of voice as you would to a friend, with the quiet confidence that he will hear and answer you. If you have a friend who loves you, you know you don't need to argue with that person or use a loud voice. All you need to do is tell your friends what you need, and you know that they will do everything possible to help. So it is with Jesus. They said of Jesus, "He will not brawl or cry out, his voice is not heard in the streets, he will not break the crushed reed, or snuff the faltering wick . . ." (Mt 12:19-20). He appreciates the gentle prayer that shows confidence in his friendship more than a raised voice that demands results. In short, when you pray with your family, you can use the same tone of voice speaking to God that you use in speaking to them. You can just relax and be yourself.

Third, you will sense more than ever that somehow the life and love of Jesus flow into people when you lay your hands on them. Babies need to be held or they may develop a sickness or even wither up and die. Similarly, we will wither up spiritually and die without the infilling of God's love, which ordinarily comes to us through other people. If you truly understand that, you will be willing to spend time praying with people, sensing that something of the life and love of Jesus comes through your hand to touch and to heal.

How well I remember a priest in my community who was dying of lung cancer. He had never given any signs of being anything but an enthusiastic teacher who never displayed the warmer side of his nature. All his talk was of ideas and concepts; he was a man's man and never showed any sign of weakness. Yet, at the end, when he could no longer talk, all he wanted was for us to take turns holding his hand. It was the last thing he would have admitted needing when he stood tall and in good health. But, at the end of life, as at the beginning, we are simple enough to admit that we need the touch of someone who cares.

At that time I didn't know about healing prayer, and only saw the human dimension of his loneliness and his reaching out with his hand for help. But since then, I have come to realize the wisdom of the gospel writers who encouraged us to lay our hands upon the sick. Now I realize that the love of God flows through our hands to radiate the sick area with God's healing power, to wither up the sickness and to enliven all the healthy cells to fight the body's enemies!

Last, we recognize that there does come a time for everyone to die, and one of the simplest, most beautiful things you can do for a friend who is dying is simply to be there, holding his or her hand, caring for your friend until the moment when he or she moves from this life to the next. Often we wonder: "Should I pray for the healing of an elderly, sickly person who seems to be dying?" If you ask God in prayer whether you should pray for healing or not and are still not sure, I would recommend doing what a sister who is a nurse has discovered is most natural in the situation: She simply prays that Jesus pour his *life* into the person. Then Jesus can make the decision whether that life will lead to entering the new life which is heaven, or whether that life will heal the sick person's body and restore it to physical health. In any case, you can simply sit by the sick person's bedside, saying a prayer here or there, but mostly just holding the person's hand, picturing the life of Jesus in you flowing into your sick friend, healing and comforting.

I remember vividly when my father and my mother died — just four months apart — what a strength it was to have several Christian friends who took turns with me during the last few nights. I would not have had the strength to do it alone. Together, we could be there at that transition from this life to that new life, for the process we call death. From time to time, we would say a prayer, or read a sentence or two from the New Testament or the Psalms—but always there was someone there to put a loving hand on my mother's forehead, or to hold her hand. At such times, words do

not come easily. Only the love that brings comfort, often in silence.

Ten:
Inner Healing

Of all the healings most of us need, the deepest, the one we need most, is usually spiritual or emotional. So often when we give weekend conferences, the group is loudly praising God and seems ecstatically happy on Friday evening. Then afterwards, our team is available to pray with individuals for a blessing in any area they want. We don't offer to pray for healing after the first session. We want to begin in a positive way, praying for a blessing, leaving the heavier healings for the next day. But, over and over, as people came forward for a blessing, the happy smile disappears and they utter a cry from the heart for inner healing: "Please pray for me. I've been thinking of suicide since my husband left me;" "Please pray because I'm in great confusion. I'm a homosexual and every so often I start cruising the streets looking for someone, and I can't seem to help it;" "I'm just plain anxious and fearful. I don't know what's wrong, but I don't like being with people."

Despite that celebration a few minutes before, many in the group were suffering in very deep ways. Some of that suffering is just part of life. It comes in any normal human situation and we refer to it as the "vale of tears" that is life. Some of the suffering calls for repentance and a change in the person's way of life. But a large part of the suffering results from the emotional wounds of the past which Jesus came to heal so that we might become a "new creation" (2 Cor 5:17).

To me, the greatest discovery in the healing ministry has been that Jesus *commonly* heals these deep wounds.

> The spirit of the Lord Yahweh
> is on me

for Yahweh has anointed me.

He has sent me to bring the news
to the afflicted,

to soothe the broken-hearted.
(Isaiah 61:1)

So far as I know, it was the late Agnes Sanford who was the first to discover, in a practical way, how Jesus might actually heal these wounds, for he had walked back with her into her past and healed her of the mental depression which, like the years of the locust, had kept her bound for seven years.

What we have discovered for ourselves (it is already there in Scripture) is that every part of Jesus, every aspect of his own emotional and mental makeup died with him upon the cross for our redemption. He was a human being like us in everything except sin.

F or the high priest we have is not incapable of feeling our weaknesses with us, but has been put to the test in exactly the same

> way as ourselves, apart from sin.
> Let us, then, have no fear in
> approaching the throne of grace to
> receive mercy and to find grace
> when we are in need of help.
> (Hebrews 4:15-16)

When Jesus cried out "I thirst," something in him was dying so that the alcoholic might not thirst again. When he cried on the cross, "My God, why have you deserted me?" he suffered the loss of his Father so that we might know the Father's presence: "We shall come to him and make a home in him" (Jn 14:23).

For all the interior weaknesses that we have, Jesus promises us a share of his own life and personality. We are meant to share in his love for his Father and his people; we are meant to share in his joy and in his peace. We are not just to try to be peaceful with him as model. We can also ask for his peace as a gift, beyond anything we can achieve by all our discipline and effort: "Peace I bequeath to you, my own peace I give you, a peace which the world cannot give, this is my gift to you" (Jn 14:27). This is not to say we don't need to try to do as much as we can to love, to be at peace, to be joyful, to be patient, but beyond a point we are bound to fail unless we ask for them as gifts, for they are fruits of the Holy Spirit.

Because of our fallen, wounded condition as human beings, we all find ourselves in the sad situation described by St. Paul: "I do not understand my own behavior; I do not act as I mean to, but I do things that I hate" (Rom 7:15). The good news is that all this compulsive activity can be healed. The completion of healing usually takes time, but often we experience quantum leaps of healing as we pray.

The study of psychology is helpful in discovering the roots of our sickness and how the evil in people and in the world twists our personalities. But while psychology is helpful in the human analysis of our problems, it is not so helpful in the cure. With the help of Jesus, however, we can get at the childhood wounds that hinder our growth and compel us to act in ways that we know are wrong but can't seem to help. I find that almost always when we have time to pray with a person over a course of time, wonderful changes begin to take place.

Just take the following statement from a woman we prayed with last month:

> It seems to me that when darkness reigns within, you do not realize what it's like to be free. Well, I feel great. All my life, a mocking ring sounded whenever I tried to love the Lord or carry out my tasks in life. The last time I heard it was just before the spirit of rejection was cast out.[1] The result—I feel good about my decisions and myself. The other day an angry woman came at me and, for the first time, her anger never touched me. Wow! It's like being in a dream and hoping that the peace I experience is for real . . . and forever.

Socializing has always been an agony for me. But now I feel good about parties and being with people. (I used to make up any excuse in any situation to get away from people.)

One of the greatest changes in me is a new vitality. I do not feel tired all the time. My whole life has been a war against fatigue . . . finding fast and easy ways to do my work so that when weariness came, I would be free to rest (sometimes 12 hours a day). Oh, do I feel good!

For myself, I have needed inner healing, mostly in the area of fear of people—a common affliction in our society. I grew up in a competitive atmosphere and I learned to compete in studies, in popularity and in sports. Like most people, I often failed. As a 135-pound, 6-foot-3-inch high school graduate, I was gawky and awkward and carried a deep inner shyness and embarrassment for years and even after I gained a little more weight. It was only through prayer that I was released so that I could more or less forget myself, and go about my work without being so self-conscious. Like me, most people carry around deep-seated fears or bitterness that prevent them from having the freedom that belongs to the children of God.

How can we go about praying for that inner freedom that we so much desire and need?

Well, there are some simple ways that can help most of us, although the more difficult cases may need the help of someone specially gifted in prayer, or a professional counselor, or, preferably, someone who combines both a special gift in prayer and professional training.

The simplest, most basic way of receiving inner healing is to ask a friend who is close to the Lord to help you. (Ideally, this would be your husband or your wife, or perhaps your mother or your father, or a member of your community.) Then set aside a time, an hour or so, when you will not be rushed.

Next, share whatever area of your life that needs to be healed. Talk about when the problem started (if you know), the key incidents in your life that caused it, and how other people may have contributed to the problem. (For instance, we are discovering that an extraordinary number of women were molested as young girls, sometimes by fathers or brothers, and this leaves deep scars that later affect their relationships with their husbands.) Share with your prayer partner, as best you can, that area of your life, together with the roots of the problem. These roots often go very far back into childhood or, occasionally, even before birth.[2] Most of these wounds go back to specific incidents or to relationships that went wrong. Relationships with fathers and mothers and embarrassing incidents in school seem especially common sources of these wounds.

For most of us, it is very difficult to share in depth about ourselves and our weaknesses. Many people cry when they vividly remember the painful days of the past. But it is healing even to be able to bring yourself to the point of sharing these experiences in depth with one or two other persons. It is a great sign of trust to be able to tell another person the truth about your life. For me, to talk is a source of strength. And for you to listen heals me on the human level. We condemn ourselves so deeply that we are helped by having someone listen who does not condemn us, but simply listens.

> Jesus was left alone with the woman, who remained in the middle. Jesus again straightened up and said, "Woman, where are they? Has no one condemned you?" "No one, sir" she replied. "Neither do I condemn you," said Jesus. "Go away, and from this moment sin no more" (Jn 8: 9-11).

Because it is so painful to share these memories and because it takes time to even try, many married people have never shared themselves at this deepest level. As a result they don't really understand each other. When one of those raw nerves that were exposed in early childhood is touched, the explosion of pain or anger that results cannot be understood without understanding the source. If those of you who are married would only set aside time to be with each other and to share your lives, and to pray together, it would help immeasurably in knowing each other and in healing each other so those flawed relationships of the past can no longer harm your life together.

Ideally, your sharing would be with a person with whom you can be totally honest, someone who will understand if you break down and cry, and who knows that crying is healthy and who would also know that you might need to be held if you cry. Clearly though, there could be difficulties if an unmarried man and woman were praying alone in this situation. So for a single person, it is often best to go to an understanding married couple for prayer. (I have seen a great deal of healing go on when individuals were held while they cried, so it is good to be in a situation where this can happen without the danger of its being misunderstood or abused in a sexual way.) I realize that you may not know or trust someone well enough to open up to them in prayer. But, I want to share the ideal in case it might be possible for you.

After you have shared as best and as deeply as you can about that area of your life that still has the power to affect you harmfully, then it is time to pray. This prayer relies on two things:

1) that Jesus was a human being like you, and that his humanity suffered in that very area where you need healing so that you might be healed;

2) that Jesus can walk back into the past and change its effects upon your present life in a way that neither you nor any psychiatrist can.

So, your friend can pray for you—or you can pray for your friend—asking Jesus to walk back and take the poison out of your past. (It is very much like the prayer we described in the chapter on forgiveness.) A simple way is to ask the person you are praying for to imagine the harmful incident, and then to imagine Jesus coming into the picture, doing each of the things that would have healed the situation at that time.

The person doing the praying can either ask Jesus to come into the picture and then be *silent while Jesus takes over and does those things that are necessary* (he really seems to do this in a certain number of cases—and these are the best, for healing always takes place). Or, the person praying can be sensitive to the inspiration of the Holy Spirit, and *pray out loud* and *describe* the various things that Jesus would do if he had been present.

The following examples will give you an idea of some of the ways Jesus heals.

Once a woman prayed for her own healing because she had experienced a very unhappy childhood dominated by a cold and critical mother who made life miserable for her at home. In the prayer, Jesus appeared and took the little girl into the laundry room where she had received many scoldings, and simply talked and sang with her and helped her fold the wash. He totally transformed that miserable memory of her home by spending a long time helping her to enjoy her work—something she had not been able to do (not simply the laundry, but all her work).

Another time I was praying with a man who felt distant from God as the result of a harsh religious education. While we prayed, Jesus appeared to him as he remembered seeing him in a picture on the wall of his childhood bedroom—seated and surrounded by little children, some on his lap, some on the ground. In the beginning of this vision he, as a boy, was seated on the ground, looking away from Jesus, for this was how he felt—alone and rejected. Then Jesus picked him up and set him on his lap, turning him around in the process. As he faced him, Jesus smiled and all feelings of rejection and distance from God dissolved.

I give you these two very simple examples because they show what I have observed about the way Jesus works: He often heals the *undramatic* hurts so many people have experienced, such as painful loneliness, as well as healing the dramatic calamities that usually dominate the testimonies at prayer meetings. When he heals, he often uses very simple, everyday ways of being present such as setting a child on his lap or helping a person work at a humdrum task.

Praying for inner healing, then, can be very simple. Just sit down next to the other person and put your hand on the person's shoulder or hand. Then ask Jesus to go back and heal each wounded relationship, each painful incident. Pray either in silence, letting Jesus do it all or, with God's inspiration, pray out loud describing how Jesus would act to make the person whole.

As you gain experience, you may also wish to ask God the *Father* to walk back and help if the person you are praying for had a broken relationship with his or her father. For Catholics especially, we find that Jesus often sends his mother Mary who, in her humanity, can make up for whatever was missing in the person's relationship with the mother.

It is very hard to tell you how to do this, because each person you pray with is so different. It is a mistake to imply that any formula prayer can cover the multitude of ways in which God's people have been wounded and the widely different ways that God himself goes about healing them. To explain how to do that in this chapter would be difficult, if not impossible. But if you realize that the idea of inner healing is very simple, if you realize that inner healing almost always takes place (more often than physical healing), you should be encouraged to pray for the people closest to you. Just listen to your friend's problem and, without pretending to analyze or judge or figure it out, begin to pray in simple ways, following the lead of the Spirit. You may find yourself picturing Jesus helping in all kinds of ways that you know you would never have thought of on your own. Most of the ways Jesus heals are very simple: He forgives people, he looks them in the eye, and the way he looks at them heals the ancient rejection; he holds them in his arms like a brother and the loneliness melts away.

One way he heals is remarkably simple: Many parents know that they have harmed their children's spiritual or emotional growth because of something they once did or said. Yet, the parents may not be able to voice the problem to the child without making it worse. If they pray in tongues, though, the mother and father can simply put their hands upon the child while the child is asleep, then pray in tongues and ask God to use the prayer to bring inner healing. Several parents I know have tried this very simple method and found dramatic changes in the child's attitude and actions the very next day!

In fact, the whole idea of praying for inner healing is so simple that we may reject it: "Such a complicated, deep-rooted problem can't be changed by such a simple prayer!" But over and over again I have seen it happen.

So share your past history with your spouse, your family or a close friend, and ask Jesus to bring his healing to the deepest recesses of the heart. He alone can bring you the peace that the world cannot give.

Epilogue

I hope by now you are encouraged to put into practice some of these very simple suggestions; they can change your life. I trust also that you will see Jesus do wonderful things in and through you. It is all so remarkably simple that it's hard to understand why more Christians have not been doing it; basically, all it involves is

—having compassion and love for people,

—believing that Jesus has far more compassion than you do (as well as the power to do something about it),

—speaking to Jesus and asking him to heal,

—and resting your hands upon the sick.

The Prayer That Heals

You have nothing to lose (other than pride) by trying, and a whole new world will open up for you in which you will see God's compassion at work.

My prayer for you is this:

Lord Jesus, give faith and confidence to the ones who read these words, so that they will want to reach out their hands to their friends. Help them to pray that pain will disappear and sickness will be healed. Give them wisdom to know how best to pray; fill their prayers with the faith that heals and their hands with the power that gives life and comfort. As they launch out and begin to pray with their families and friends, let them know you more deeply than ever before. Let them experience the wonder and intimacy of the friend you are: Jesus Christ, our Lord, our healer and our friend.

Amen.

Endnotes

Introduction

1. This percentage is *remarkably* consistent in all parts of the United States; the hands raised are seldom over 5%. The only exception was among the students at Oral Roberts University where about 50% could remember their fathers praying with them. On the other hand, at one retreat for 100 seminarians not a single one could remember his father ever praying with him. (Small wonder, then, that after ordination they may have difficulty feeling comfortable leading people in spontaneous prayer.) I have asked the same question in various other countries with much the same results. At one gathering of 2,000 people in Korea, only one hand went up.

2. Barbara Shlemon's *Healing Prayer* (Ave Maria Press) and Agnes Sanford's *Healing Light* (Logos International) are two fine books I have handed

out to many friends who wanted a sound, simple book on how to pray for the sick.

Chapter Two

1. The relationship of the sacrament of confirmation with the baptism of the Spirit is a much-discussed topic, but there is no need to go into it here. I do know that God has used the prayers of little children who are baptized but not confirmed to heal their parents. Yet, there seems to be an added power to minister and heal that comes with the baptism of the Spirit.

Chapter Three

1. Since 1981 when I wrote this book, the practice of praying together has notably improved, especially in the independent, evangelical churches.

Chapter Four

2. Judith and I have written a book, *Praying for Your Unborn Child* which describes this beautiful practice. It can be obtained by ordering it from

the bookstore at Christian Healing Ministries, P.O. Box 9520, Jacksonville, FL 32208.

Chapter Five

1. It is significant, I think, that in the United States, most mainline Protestant churches are either losing members or just holding steady, while Pentecostal and Evangelical churches, where the personal expression of faith is encouraged, are growing rapidly. (The Roman Catholic Church has a slow growth in numbers which is roughly equivalent to the population growth.) A good case can be made that where Christians do not experience a personal relationship with Jesus Christ, they will have little desire to share their faith with others—or to pray with others. Men especially are afraid of "emotionalism" and use that as an excuse not to pray in a personal way.

Chapter Six

1. Catholics might wish to pray the rosary.

Chapter Seven

1. Here I would especially recommend reading *Feeling and Healing Your Emotions* by Dr. Conrad Baars (Logos International).

2. Because the Gospel speaks so much about forgiveness, many Christians feel guilty about feeling angry. Yet Jesus was very angry at times, as when he called the Pharisees a "brood of vipers." Paul says we should be angry but not sin. Anger is a good, God-given emotion. But we must choose an appropriate action to work out our anger and at the appropriate time, we must forgive.

Chapter Eight

1. Dr. Charles Farah, Jr., has written a book on this subject. *From the Pinnacle of the Temple: Faith vs. Presumption* (Logos International), in which he goes into the dangers of identifying faith with a readiness to claim healing without a special inspiration from God.

2. In my book, *Healing* (Ave Maria Press), chapter 18 is a discussion of the reasons people are not healed.

Chapter Nine

1. A fascinating book on this subject, *Treating Type A Behavior and Your Heart* by Meyer Friedman, M.D. (Fawcett-Crest), is excellent reading if you have had heart problems or if you are the typically American competitive type of person.

Chapter Ten

1. Along with the inner healing there was also some deliverance from evil spirits.

2. In the actual praying, several people I know suddenly found themselves re-experiencing things they did not consciously remember—impressions going back to the time when they were carried in their mother's womb. Occasionally, a grown man will fall to the floor, start crying and cry out, " I am not coming out! I don't want to be born!" You suddenly realize that he is reliving a painful time before birth and we need to pray to free him from these painful memories that still touch his adult life. Experiences like these have helped me realize, even more deeply than before, the tragedy of abortion.

Born in St. Louis, Mo., in 1925, Francis MacNutt became a pre-med student but was drafted and served as an army surgical technician in World War II. He later received a B.A. from Harvard University and an M.F.A. from Catholic University of America, where he decided to enter the Roman Catholic priesthood. After becoming a member of the Dominican order and being ordained as a priest in 1956, he earned a Ph.D. in theology and he was appointed to teach Homiletics (preaching) in the Dominican Seminary. During his seven years of teaching, Francis wrote three books on preaching and was elected president of the Catholic Homiletic Society.

In 1967, Francis experienced the Baptism of the Holy Spirit and learned about praying for healing from Rev. Tommy Tyson and

Agnes Sanford at a life-changing conference in Tennessee. He became one of the first Roman Catholics to become involved in the charismatic renewal movement. In 1968, he helped start a prayer group in St. Louis. By the late '60s, the demand for teaching about charismatic renewal grew so great that he resigned his administrative positions and went into a full-time preaching ministry that led him to 31 countries in all five continents. As a home base, Francis established Merton House in St. Louis, and was a founder of the Association of Christian Therapists in 1976.

In 1975, Francis met Judith Sewell in Jerusalem and five years later they married and settled in Clearwater, Fla. Together they founded Christian Healing Ministries and traveled widely, speaking as a team and taking their two children with them. In 1987 they moved to Jacksonville, Florida, invited there by the Episcopal Diocese of Florida, and since then, their center has continued to grow. In 1993, they received a dispensation to marry from the Roman Catholic Church.

In 1974, Francis wrote Healing, which has become a classic and sold nearly a million copies in the United States alone. He also has written Power to Heal, Overcome by The Spirit, Deliverance from Evil Spirits, Homosexuality: Can It Be Healed?, and The Nearly Perfect Crime: How the Church Nearly Killed the Ministry of Healing. He and Judith co-authored Praying For Your Unborn Child. Francis continues speaking, teaching and writing, and he and Judith serve as founding directors of Christian Healing Ministries.